X-PRESIDENTS, No. 279, Sept. 2000. By Robert Smigel and Adam McKay. Published monthly by RANDOM HOUSE COMICS GROUP, Random Blvd., New York, N.Y. 10001. Seymour Fannenbaun, Editor. Bob McAdoo, Editorial Director. My Son-in-law, Waste of Space. SECOND CLASS POSTAGE PAID AT SPARTA, Ill. under the Find Some Use For Sparta, Ill. Act of March 3, 1874. Subscriptions: U.S., $19.95 for 12 issues. CANADA, $85.95 for 12 issues. Screw you, Canada. We don't want you. All other foreign, eat me. You're not getting a copy. For advertising rates address Richard A Lehman & Co., New York, N.Y. Tell them you'd like to advertise and would like to know the rates. Ask them if there's a way the rates could be sent to you, or perhaps just read over the phone. Better yet, let me call. You'll just fuck it up. Copyright National Broadcasting Casserole, Inc. 1997. All rights reserved under the Pan-American and Sino American Copyright Conventions and Slave Trade Cooperations. The stories, characters, and incidents mentioned in this magazine are absolutely hilarious. Kudos to all involved. No actual persons, living or dead, will buy this book.

X PRESIDENTS

CHAPTER 1 — THE ORIGIN

THEY WERE NOT ALWAYS THE POWERFUL HEROES WE KNOW TODAY. THE LIFE OF A FORMER PRESIDENT CAN BE A LONELY ONE . . .

NO LONGER NEEDED BY SOCIETY . . . SCORNED BY THE FICKLE PUBLIC . . . AND COLDLY SCRUTINIZED BY THE ULTIMATE JUDGE . . . *HISTORY.*

GOING FISHING AGAIN TODAY, DEAR?

OH, YEAH, BAR! ANOTHER GREAT DAY FOR FISHING! JUST LIKE YESTERDAY WAS! MAYBE EVEN BETTER THAN THE DAY *BEFORE* YESTERDAY!

HOW ARE THE MEMOIRS GOING, DEAR?

GOIN' GREAT GUNS!

My name is George Bush. I

YOU HAVE NO NEW MESSAGES. FOR OLD MESSAGES, PRESS ONE.

FIRST OLD MESSAGE. SENT NOVEMBER 4, 1992. 3:40 A.M.

HI, GEORGE. THIS IS DAN QUAYLE. SORRY ABOUT THE ELECTION.

FINAL OLD MESSAGE.

NO ONE HAS CALLED YOU SINCE NOVEMBER 4, 19 - -

OTHER FORMER PRESIDENTS, MORE ACCESSIBLE TO SOCIETY, STILL FIND *HUMILIATION* AT EVERY CORNER.

YO.

YO, MAN, I *KNOW* YOU!

HI, HOW ARE YOU?

WELL, PERHAPS IF --

I KNOW YOU YOU'RE THAT PRESIDENT! YOU'RE CARTER, RIGHT?

WELL, YES, I

YOU FUCKED UP THAT HOSTAGE SHIT!

WELL, IT WAS A --

WITH THE *AYATOLLAH*, RIGHT?

MAN, THAT WAS FUCKED UP!

WELL, IT WAS A DIFFIC --

YO, MAN, WHY YOU BUGGIN' THAT OLD GUY?

WHO?

YO MAN, THAT'S *CARTER*!

THAT'S CARTER, MAN, HE WAS, LIKE *PRESIDENT*, AND SHIT, AND HE FUCKED IT UP!

OOOH, DAMN!

WELL, THAT'S KIND OF A SIMPLIFI --

YO, CARTER, I GOTTA GET YOUR AUTOGRAPH! *SELL* THAT SHIT! DAMN, I DON'T GOT NOTHIN' TO SIGN!

OH. WELL --

YO, SIGN THE BAG!

YEAH, YEAH! SIGN THE BAG!

WELL, ALRIGHT, I GUESS I COULD . . .

COOL.

Best Timmy

OKAY, AND YOUR NAME IS --

-- OH --

OH SHIT!

RI-IIP

FOOL! YOU GOTTA *PAY* FOR THAT SHIT!

3

4

AND FOR SOME FORMER PRESIDENTS, ECLIPSED IN POPULARITY BY THEIR OWN WIVES, THE UNKINDEST CUT OF ALL . . .

WELCOME TO THE *Betty Ford* CENTER

KELSEY! KEITH! COME IN! I'M SO PROUD OF YOU BOTH!

HELLO, DARLING!

WE LOVE YOU, BETTY.

I LOVE *YOU!*

HAVE YOU MET MACKENZIE PHILLIPS?

HI-

AND JOEY LAWRENCE . . .

DELIGHTED . .

CAN I GET A SANDWICH?

WHO'S THE GUY?

OH, THAT'S MY HUSBAND, GERRY.

HELLO, GERRY.

HI.

SO, WHAT DO YOU DO, GERRY?

UH . . . GOLF . . . I LIKE GOLF.

GREAT.

GERRY USED TO BE THE PRESIDENT.

FANTASTIC. CAN YA GET SOME COFFEE, TERRY?

I'LL SHOW THEM . . .

I'LL SHOW THEM ALL . . .

5

6

. . . UNTIL ONE DAY THAT WOULD FOREVER CHANGE THEIR LIVES-- AND THE COURSE OF HISTORY!

MILTON BERLE CELEBRITY SENIOR PRO - AM LOVE CANAL NY

YOU SUCK!

FUCK ME!

WAIT. TRISHA YEARWOOD AND I WANT TO PLAY THROUGH.

OH. SORRY, SUGAR RAY.

I'LL SHOW THEM . . . I'LL SHOW 'EM . . . SO HELP ME . . . I HATE CARTER . . . I'M MORE THAN JUST A FOOTNOTE . . . I WON THE COLD WAR . . . TRISHA YEARWOOD LOOKED OLDER THAN I PICTURED . . .

BOO! ZIP HISS!

BOO! HISS!

POW

7

SUDDENLY, MOTHER NATURE AND FATHER RADIATION HAVE THEIR EMPHATIC SAY . . .

I LIKE GETTING CARRIED AWAY SOMETIMES, BUT THIS IS *RIDICULOUS!*

HE'LL BE MISSED.

YES.

WHAT'S HAPPENING?

WHAT?

CAN'T HEAR!

WHERE IS EVERYONE?

DUNNO. LETS PLAY.

FEEL . . . *DIFFERENT* SOMEHOW . . .

8

SOMETHING . . . *HAPPENING* . . . TO ME . . .

CAN'T SHAKE . . . FEELING . . .

DON'T . . . UNDERSTAND . . . WHEN THE LIGHTNING HIT, IT MUST'VE . . . SEEM DIFFERENT . . . STILL HATE CARTER . . . PLAYING GOLF . . . TOO WELL . . .

CONFUSED AND AFRAID, THEY AGREE TO MEET LATER AT A MORE PRIVATE SETTING, A PLACE OF SOLITUDE WHERE HUMANS NEVER VENTURE . . .

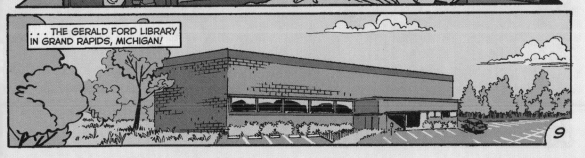

. . . THE GERALD FORD LIBRARY IN GRAND RAPIDS, MICHIGAN!

9

ONCE AGAIN WE'VE BEEN GIVEN EXTRAORDINARY POWERS.

YES. FIRST BY THE VOTERS, AND NOW BY RADIOACTIVE LIGHTNING.

WE'VE GOT TO FIGURE OUT WHAT TO DO WITH THESE TALENTS.

HELL, YEAH. WE CAN MAKE A FORTUNE WITH THIS. START AN *ACT*, TAKE IT ON THE ROAD.

YOU SHOULD REA[D] BOOK[S]

I'VE STILL GOT THE BUG.

WHAT ARE YOU TALKING ABOUT? WE'VE GOT THE POWER TO DO *ANYTHING* HERE!

CARTER'S RIGHT. WHY BOTHER WITH AN ACT? WE'RE STRONGER THAN PEOPLE. WE CAN HIT THEM IN THE HEAD AND TAKE THEIR MONEY.

NOT BAD, FORD . . .

NO! NO! I'M TALKING ABOUT HELPING PEOPLE! USING OUR POWERS TO HELP MAKE THE WORLD BETTER!

I'LL BE HONEST. I COULD USE THE SCRATCH.

I'M WITH YA.

ME TOO.

CAN'T WE GIVE SOME OF THE MONEY TO THE HOMELESS?

I'M GOING TO KICK YOUR ASS IN A SECOND.

YOU SHOULD READ BOOKS

LET'S PLAY *LAS VEGAS*!

I KNOW A GUY AT *SIX FLAGS* WE COULD AUDITION FOR! WE COULD MAKE A MINT!

LISTEN! WE CAN'T START OFF TOO BIG! THERE'S A CARNIVAL OFF ROUTE 12 NEAR MY HOUSE. HANDS IN!

QUIT SULKING, CARTER! THAT'S WHAT COST YOUR ASS A SECOND TERM!

YOU SHOULD 2 BOOKS

TO THE ROADSIDE CARNIVAL!

AND SO, OUR FORMER PRESIDENTS SET OFF ON THEIR QUEST FOR FAME AND FORTUNE . . .

. . . ARMED WITH A NEW ATTITUDE AND A NEW NAME!

NOT BAD. WHAT DO YOU CALL YOURSELVES?

THE AWESOME BOYS!

IT'S SIX SHOWS A DAY, TEN BUCKS A SHOW. INJURE YOURSELF ON THE JOB, IT'S YOUR PROBLEM. YOU SMOKE DOPE, THAT'S COOL, JUST DON'T DO IT ON CARNIVAL GROUNDS AND MAKE SURE YOU SAVE A TOKE FOR ME! HEH, HEH, HEH.

SOMEHOW, I THINK WE COULD'VE DONE BETTER.

YOU SHOULD HAVE SAID THAT IN IRAQ. NOW WHO WANTS A FUNNEL CAKE?

I DO.

11

SOMEBODY STOP HIM!

WHAT WAS THAT?

I THINK SOMEBODY STOLE A WHITESNAKE MIRROR!

THIS IS GOOD.

ALL YOU HAD TO DO WAS DELAY HIM FOR A SECOND!

WE'RE OFF THE CLOCK, FELLA!

I'M GLAD I DIDN'T VOTE FOR ANY OF YOU!

YEAH? WHO'D YOU VOTE FOR? JOHN ANDERSON?

HA HA HA HA HA HA

HA HA HA HA HA HA HA HA

WHACK THE FROG

AND SO BEGINS A RAPID RETURN TO RENOWN! ROADSIDE CARNIVALS . . .

RENAISSANCE FAIRS . . .

12

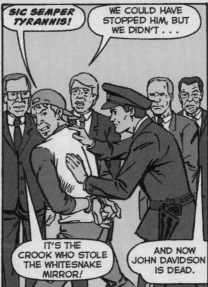

13

YOU MUST BUILD A FORTRESS CONTAINING SECRET HEADQUARTERS . . . AND FROM NOW ON, YOU MUST CALL YOURSELVES *"X-PRESIDENTS."*

ALSO YOU MUST CARPET BOMB CAMBODIA.

TO FIGHT INJUSTICE . . .

WITHOUT A HITCH . . .

TO HELP THE HELPLESS . . .

BY HELPING THE RICH!

X-PRESIDENTS!

RIGHTING WRONGS, SOLVING PROBLEMS BIG AND SMALL, FROM WASHINGTON TO WYOMING, THE X-PRESIDENTS STRIVE TO MAKE AMERICA GREAT AND THE REST OF THE WORLD ALMOST AS GOOD!

14

CHAPTER 2 EVIL SWEARS IN

FOR OUR HEROES, FAME IS NOT ONLY RECAPTURED, BUT MULTIPLIED.

NOW IT'S EVERY BOY'S DREAM TO BE AN **X-PRESIDENT!**

I WANNA GROW UP, BE *PRESIDENT*, DO WHATEVER, THEN GET HIT BY RADIATION AND BE AN *X-PRESIDENT!*

BUT NOT EVERYONE PAINTS A ROSY X-PRESIDENTIAL PORTRAIT! WITNESS THE LIBERAL MEDIA!

... I'M INSPIRED BY THEIR HEROICS --

OH, COME ON, GEORGE! FOUR OF OUR GREAT WORLD LEADERS ARE REDUCED TO *COMMON VIGILANTES!*

SAM, THESE MEN ARE SAVING PEOPLE FROM DROIDS!

17

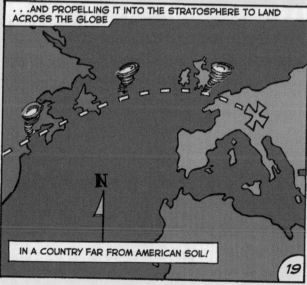

GOOD WORK, BUSH! YOU REALLY STAYED THE COURSE!

THANKS, GIPPER!

RIGHT, SNOOKUMS?

MOLE PEOPLE!

CONFRONTED WITH THE TREACHERY OF MOLE PEOPLE DISGUISED AS AMERICAN BABIES, THE X-PRESIDENTS COMBINE THEIR MIGHT TO FORCE THE MOLE PEOPLE BACK TO THEIR SUB-EARTH DWELLINGS!

WE'VE GOT TO KEEP THE PUBLIC CALM! SO LET ME HANDLE THIS!

NOW, NOW! WE'RE GOING TO TRY TO GET TO ALL OF YOUR QUESTIONS! YES, BILL FROM NEWSWEEK . . .

IS IT TRUE THAT YOU BEAT UP INFANTS?

NOW COME ON BILL! HAVE YOU EVER HAD TO CHANGE A BABY'S DIAPERS?

HA HA HA HA HA HA HA HA HA HA

21

22

BUT WHAT ABOUT THE *MOLEBAB* --

HOLD ON . . . THINKING ALOUD . . . MOLES -- MO-AMAR . . .

KHADDAFI *AND* REPTILIO?

. . . AXES . . .

. . . HATCHET . . .

. . . *HUSSEIN!* . . . I HATE CARTER . . . EVIL . . .

ELECTROBRAIN! COULD IT BE . . . ?

A WORLDWIDE CONSPIRACY TO REVIVE COMMUNISM! FORD -- TAKE A MOLEBABY FOR EXAMINATION! TO THE *LAIR-BRARY!*

SOMEWHERE IN THE THIRD WORLD . . .

YOU CALL THOSE MOLE PEOPLE? THEY SUBMITTED SO QUICKLY!

YOU VILLAINS SHOULD HAVE SPRUNG FOR *PUREBRED* MOLE PEOPLE!

WE'RE NOT MADE OF MONEY!

UNITED VILLAINS FOR THE **OVERTHROW** OF **AMERICA**

IDI AMIN'S RIGHT!

BURP!

OF COURSE YOU DON'T HAVE MONEY, MRS. MARCOS! YOU'VE *SPENT* IT ON SHOES!

WE'RE NOT FOOLS! WE WATCH JAY LENO!

WELL SAID, REPTILIO! WE'RE WORKING WITH *IMBECILES!*

ខ្ញុំមិនដែលបានអាក់អន់ ចិត្តយ៉ាងខ្លាំងម្ដងឡើយ!

POL POT'S BRAIN SAYS HE'S NEVER BEEN MORE OFFENDED!

POL POT

YOU EVIL GENIUSES AREN'T EXACTLY LIGHTING UP THE SKY! WHAT ABOUT THAT *SPY* YOU SENT?

23

IT APPEARS THE RECEPTOR SPY DECOY RECEIVED INSUFFICIENT INFORMATION!

HELLO, EVERYONE.

WHAT'S WRONG?

QUIET, HUSSEIN! I'M READING ITS CHIP.

WHICH ONE OF YOU IS THE SHY ONE? *I WAS NEVER GOOD ENOUGH FOR MOM!* A TWISTER'S JUST HIT AN AXE FACTORY! *WE'VE GOTTA GO!* I UNDERSTAND.

ELECTROBRAIN! IT WAS YOUR JOB TO TIME THE *TORNADO!* I MUST EAT YOU!

LET'S NOT QUIBBLE! WE MUST *STOP* THE X-PRESIDENTS BEFORE THEY TRACK US DOWN!

X-PRESIDENT HEADQUARTERS . . .

KYGEN
SULPHUR
$(\frac{9}{10} \times \sqrt{4})$
$\Delta 57^3 - X^2$

LET'S GET A READOUT ON A-42.

ROGER.

RRRINNNG
RKRINNNG

I THINK WE'LL FIND THESE MOLE AUTOPSY RESULTS VERY INTERESTING.

COULD YOU ANSWER THAT, HAIG?

HELLO?

24

IN SEARCH OF THE HIDEOUT, X-PRESIDENTS CARTER AND BUSH PLUNGE DEEP INTO THE MYSTERIOUS WATERS OF THE CHARLES RIVER!

OPENING DAY
MEET AND GREET
MICHAEL DUKAKIS

BOSTON SEAQUARIUM

BI BLIKKA BLEE BAMON!*

BLEBO, BLUB!*

* I THINK I SEE A SALMON!

* LET'S GO, BUSH!

HA! THE TRAP IS WORKING!

I JOIN YOU IN YOUR EVIL! A TOAST!

UNIT VILLAINS
DE FOR THE
OW

POL POT BRAIN

26

BLOLY BLILLIE BLORBON! *

* HOLY WILLIE HORTON!

. . . LIKE THE SLOW BUILD-UP OF CORAL OVER TIME, THE ERECTION OF THIS SEAQUARIUM AND GIFT SHOP IS A TESTIMONY TO . . .

BOSTON SEAQUA...

CHRIST, DUKAKIS. TELL A FOOTBALL STORY OR SOMETHING . . .

LET'S LEAVE RESPECTFULLY!

UH-OH! TROUBLE!

WITH THE OTHERS IN PERIL, X-PRESIDENT FORD DRAWS UPON HIS ABILITY TO COMMUNICATE WITH THE CREATURES OF THE SEA . . .

WHOOP WHOOP WHOOP

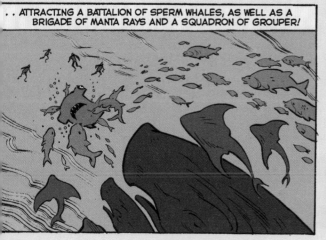

. . ATTRACTING A BATTALION OF SPERM WHALES, AS WELL AS A BRIGADE OF MANTA RAYS AND A SQUADRON OF GROUPER!

BLEE BLEMMER BLEAT BLEBLOWIC. *

BLEAH. *

IS THAT A WIG?

* WE WILL NEVER FORGET YOUR GLORIOUS HEROICS.

* YEAH.

27

28

REAGAN RANCH . . .

THANKS FOR COMING BACK.

A PLEASURE.

WHAT MAKES THE X-PRESIDENTS HAPPY?

HAPPY? HAPPY?

HAPPY? HAPPY?

CAREFUL, CARTER, IT'S A BOMB!

KA-BOOM!

AAAAAARGHHH! THEY GOT AWAY!

AMIN! I TOLD YOU EATING THE SERBIAN WOULDN'T SOLVE ANYTHING!

THEY'VE SEPARATED TO FEND US OFF! THESE X-PRESIDENTS ARE CLEVERER THAN WE THOUGHT!

THEY'RE TOO QUICK! TOO POWERFUL!

THERE IS ANOTHER WAY! WE SHALL DESTROY THEIR *CREDIBILITY!*

YES! NOT EVEN AN *X*-AMERICAN PRESIDENT IS IMPERVIOUS TO SCANDAL!

IT'S TRUE! AMERICANS HAVE SUCH *UNREASONABLY HIGH STANDARDS* FOR THEIR LEADERS -- AS WELL AS FOR EVERYTHING ELSE!

ON THAT WE ALL AGREE! BUT CAN WE *CRACK* AN X-PRESIDENT'S WILL?

IF WE SEND THE BAIT, THEY'LL BITE!

MRS. MARCOS . . . YOUR EVIL IS EXCEEDED ONLY BY YOUR . . . ALLURE.

THIS IS FANTASTIC! BUT WHICH X-PRESIDENT SHALL WE REEL IN FIRST?

I THINK WE KNOW WHICH IS THE WEAKEST!

SOMEWHERE IN ATLANTA . . .

MR. PRESIDENT, I'M GONNA GO DOWNSTAIRS AND GET SOME SHINGLES.

ALRIGHT, THEO. I THINK WE'RE RUNNING LOW ON CAULK, TOO.

I'LL TAKE CARE OF IT MR. PRESIDENT.

THANKS. AND PLEASE CALL ME JIMMY. WE'RE ALL THE SAME HERE.

HABITAT FOR HUMANITY

ALRIGHT, SIR.

OR EVEN BETTER, CALL ME JIMBO.

OKAY!

HABITAT FOR HUMANITY

MY . . . I SEEM TO HAVE DROPPED MY IRON STICKS . . .

32

33

SHE'S GOT HIM!

PERFECT! HUSSEIN! ALERT THE LIBERAL MEDIA!

UNITED
DEDIC
OVERTHR

ANYWAY, "ZEN AND THE ART OF MOTORCYCLE MAINTENANCE" IS A GREAT BOOK IF YOU CAN FIND IT . . .

MAYBE YOU CAN BRING IT OVER SOMETIME . . .

UH . . . I'M A MARRIED MAN . . .

I WANT YOU TO BE ON ME!

I . . . OH, WELL . . .

HABITAT FOR HUMANITY

I DIDN'T NEED TO SEE THAT!

IS HE DOUBLE-JOINTED?

36

NOW, HOLD ON! MAYBE I'M OLD-FASHIONED, BUT I THINK THIS KIND OF DISPLAY IS INAPPROPRIATE, AND UNNECESSARY! I THINK STORIES SHOULD BE DONE LIKE THE *OLD DAYS*, WHEN IT WAS ALL LEFT TO THE IMAGINATION . . .

I THINK IT'S ABOUT TO RAIN!

SEE? WASN'T THAT BETTER?

MR. PRESIDENT! IT'S A *TRAP!*

YOU SEE WHAT *YOU* SEE.

NO! SIR, THAT'S *IMELDA MARCOS* IN DISGUISE!

IT IS? OH, DEAR LORD!

HEY! WHAT THE HELL'S GOING ON?

35

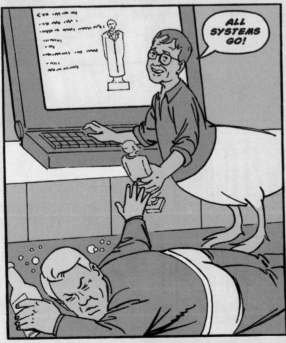

HAS THE NEBULA'S NERDIEST NATIVE JUST SAVED LIBERTY'S SACRED ASS? THE ANSWER'S RIGHT AROUND THE CORNER, MORON!

38

39

ALRIGHT, BACK TO WORK! SEARCH EVERYWHERE! COMMUNISTS ALWAYS LEAVE CLUES!

LOOKS PRETTY CLEAN, SIR!

STATUE OF LIBERTY

OH, YEAH? TAKE A GANDER! THEY ALL LEFT THEIR *NAMES!* IT'S LIKE THEY'RE TAUNTING US! AARONSON, ABONDANZA . . .

RIGHT . . . MR. REAGAN, THOSE ARE THE NAMES OF ALL THE IMMIGRANTS --

ELLIS ISLAND

EXACTLY!

NO, SIR -- THE ONES WHO CAME HERE YEARS AGO! IT'S A TRIBUTE!

YES. THEY'LL BE MISSED.

WHAT?

JUST SHUT UP!

WAIT! I THINK SOMEONE LEFT A MESSAGE HERE!

WHAT DOES IT SAY?

UH . . . I . . . UH . . .

WHAT?

I, UH . . .

FIND SMALL LENIN STATUE IN KUWAIT. IT WILL LEAD YOU TO THE HIDEOUT.

. . . FORGOT MY GLASSES . . .

YOU DON'T WEAR GLASSES.

THAT'S RIGHT . . .

IT . . . UH . . . I . . .

I CAN'T READ!

WE'RE SORRY . . .

IT'S OKAY, GERRY. I ALWAYS SUSPECTED.

41

PLEASE. HE WANTS TO BE AROUND REPUBLICANS.

WHY DON'T YOU JUST READ THE CLUE?

"FIND SMALL LENIN STATUE IN KUWAIT. IT WILL LEAD YOU TO THE HIDEOUT." WOW! WE'D BETTER GO!

YES! ONCE WE FIGURE OUT THE *RIDDLE*...

WHAT DO YOU MEAN?

"FIND SMALL LENIN STATUE IN KUWAIT..."

IT SOUNDS LIKE PRETTY SPECIFIC INSTRUCTIONS...

IT DOES!... BUT WHAT COULD IT MEAN? THOSE WILY FOREIGNERS... KUWAIT... WAIT-KU... SMALL LENIN... TINY BEATLE...

MAYBE WE SHOULD JUST FOLLOW WHAT IT SAYS --

WE'RE NOT GOING *ANYWHERE* TILL WE CRACK THIS RIDDLE! NOW THERE'S A TINY BEETLE, OR INSECT! WE KNOW *THAT*! BUT WHAT'S A WAIT-KU?

I... I DON'T KNOW.

TWO MONTHS LATER

I'VE *GOT* IT! THERE'S A SMALL STATUE OF LENIN THAT WE NEED TO GET IN KUWAIT TO GET US INTO THE HIDEOUT!

BUT THAT'S WHAT WE --

QUICK! THERE'S NO TIME TO LOSE!

42

43

44

WELL, GO AHEAD, CARTER! *WE'RE* NOT RUBBING LENIN'S FILTHY HEAD!

IT'S ACTIVATED! FOLLOW LENIN!

OKAY... JUST THIS ONCE!

THE FBI HAS NO CLUES AS TO THE WHEREABOUTS OF THE STATUE OF LIBERTY, NOR SERBIAN LEADER SLOBODAN MILOSEVIC...

HA! AMERICA'S WILL IS BROKEN!

YES! AND WE SHALL DRAW UPON LADY LIBERTY'S RESOURCES. WE SHALL MATE HER WITH ANOTHER AMERICAN ICON -- THE ONE NAMED *TED WILLIAMS!*

YOU FOOL! HE'S *NINETY!* HE COULDN'T EVEN HAVE A *CATCH* IN HIS CURRENT STATE!

BUT... HE'S TEDDY BALLGAME.

THE ANSWER IS SIMPLE. WE SHOULD CAPTURE TWENTY YOUNGER PLAYERS TO EQUAL THIS GREAT OLD ONE. HERE... GET DAVE MAGADAN, TIPPY MARTINEZ, LEE MAY...

BAKE MCBRIDE, ODDIBE MCDOWELL... SOMEONE ELSE DO THIS!

47

CAN'T . . . HANG . . . ON . . .

MUST FIND ANTIDOTE . . . REVERSE . . . COMMUNIST . . . REVIVAL . . .

YEAH . . .

THERE IS AN ANTIDOTE.

KISSINGER!

TELL US!

IT'S RIGHT INSIDE THE --

NOT RIGHT NOW.

IT'S RIGHT INSIDE NORIEGA'S TRUNK. HE LEFT IT BEHIND. YOU MUST USE IT, WITHOUT HESITATION.

WHAT IS IT?

THE ONLY KNOWN ANTIDOTE -- IS CRACK COCAINE!

WE HAVE TO SMOKE CRACK?

NO! HENRY . . . PLEASE . . . THERE MUST BE ANOTHER WAY!

HERE'S THE CRACK.

LET'S DO IT.

NO! WE WILL NOT INGEST ILLEGAL NARCOTICS!

WOW! LOOK AT THIS STASH.

IT'S YOUR DUTY, MR. REAGAN, AS A SUPER DUPER CRIME FIGHTER.

IF RONNIE'S OUT, I'M OUT!

KISS-ASS! MAYBE SOMEONE ELSE CAN CONVINCE YOU.

DO IT, DAD! IT'S REALLY NOT THAT BAD!

W! WHAT ARE YOU DOING THERE?

49

YOU KIDDING, DAD? IT'S A *KISSINGER* PARTY!

THANKS.

NOW LISTEN TO ME! THIS COUNTRY *NEEDS* YOU FELLAS! NOW YOU MARCH RIGHT UP TO THAT CRACK PIPE, TURN ON SOME STEELY DAN AND CHASE THE DRAGON BEFORE IT'S TOO LATE!

LORD FORGIVE US ALL.

NOURISHED BY THE MOTHER'S MILK OF CRACK COCAINE, OUR HEROES GAIN FAR MORE POWER AND AGGRESSION THAN IS EVEN NECESSARY!

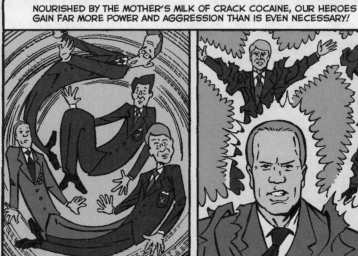

PAUSING BRIEFLY TO WORK OFF THE EXCESS, THE COMMANDERS-IN-CHIEF COME DOWN FROM THEIR HIGH AND RESTORE AMERICA AND LADY LIBERTY TO THEIR RIGHTFUL PLACES AS THE LEADERS OF ALL HUMANS AND STATUES!

50

52

AND JUST WHEN IT APPEARS OUR MONO-LITHS OF TRUTH ARE SAFE, AN UNKNOWN EVIL SETS ITS SIGHTS ON THE NEW JERUSALEM ITSELF -- *WASHINGTON, D.C.!*

LOOK, SON - IT'S GEORGE WASHINGTON!

ZAP

WOW!

WHUH?

WITH NO WARNING, OUR TALLEST AND MOST BELOVED SHAFT BECOMES A LEGGED FORCE OF UNIMAGINABLE TERROR!

IT'S THE WASHINGTON MONUMENT!

MY LORD! IT'S LEGGED! LET'S ROLL!

HA HA HA HA HA HA

WHIP INFLATION LATER, AND YOU *NOW* -- WHOA!

YOU IDIOT! YOU'VE MADE HIM MAD!

HIM?

53

54

IT WON'T NEGOTIATE! CAN WE CALL FOR HELP?

THERE'S ONLY ONE OPTION! A FORCE SO TERRIBLE IT ONCE NEARLY DESTROYED THIS WHOLE TOWN!

FLIPPING THE REANIMATING BUTTON, PRESIDENT REAGAN SENDS A SIGNAL . . .

. . .TO YORBA LINDA, CALIFORNIA, WHERE HELP IS WAITING!

I AM NOT A CROOK -- I'M A KILLING MACHINE!

CHECKERS! AWAY!

RICHARD M. NIXON 1912 - 1994

MR. REAGAN! THE DECLARATION JUST URINATED ON THE CONSTITUTION!

DISRESPECTFUL BASTARD!

I NEVER LIKED THAT DOCUMENT ANYWAY.

LET ME MAKE THIS PERFECTLY CLEAR . . . YOU'RE A PUSSY!!

I'VE GOT A DECLARATION FOR YOU, CARL: EAT SHIT!

57

SHRED 'EM BUSH! SOCK IT TO *HIM!*

BOOM!

NIXON! NOW MORE THAN EVER!!

MAKE NO MISTAKE ABOUT *THIS!*

AWAY!

WELL, OUR GREATEST MONUMENTS ARE DEAD. BUT AT LEAST THEY CAN'T HURT US.

THEY'LL BE MISSED.

BUT WE'VE STILL GOT MOUNT RUSHMORE, THE SPACE PROGRAM, AND THE LABOR DAY TELETHON.

AND I'M WORKING ON A NEW DECLARATION OF INDEPENDENCE, MR. PRESIDENT!

58

OKAY . . . COULD YOU PUT IN A CLAUSE ABOUT *THREE TERMS?*

YOU'RE FUCKIN' *NUTS!*

HA HA HA HA HA HA HA HA HA HA HA HA

BABY BABY I LOVE YA
AND I'M A BIG ASSHOLE
WE'RE ALL GREAT BIG DICKHEADS
AND WE STILL WET THE BED
COME ON EVERYBODY, SING
WE'RE BIG DICKHEADS
COME ON EVERY —

HEY, SOMEONE SWITCHED THESE LYRICS!

SOUNDS LIKE CASTRO!

NO, THESE ARE THE *WORST* KIND OF COMMUNISTS . . .

ALIENS!

COULD OUR CHERISHED COLD WAR CONQUERER BE CORRECT? DON'T STOP READING NOW OR I'LL TEAR YOUR FUCKING CHANNEL-FLIPPING NINTENDO-WORSHIPPING HEAD OFF!

59

MAIL TO THE CHIEFS

THE X-PRESIDENTIAL MAILBAG

X-PRESIDENTS ANSWER QUESTIONS FROM YOU ABOUT THEIR SUPER POWERS AND PAST ADVENTURES!

Dear X-President Bush,

You scumbag! You cut my health benefits. And you lied about the arms for hostage deal.

Signed,
**Tony Piller
Waverly, R.I.**

THANKS FOR WRITING IN, TONY!

Dear X-President Reagan,

My dad says you are a cocksucker because you supported scabs when he was an air traffic controller.

He says you are a sell-out prick.

**Rot in hell,
Betsy Stevens
Midland, Tex.**

BECAUSE WE READ YOUR LETTER, BETSY, YOU GET A FREE T-SHIRT!

Dear X-President Carter,

I resent the implication made earlier in the comic that I am a former drug-user. That's the one bad thing I'm not.

Signed,
Joey Lawrence

P.S. I like the way you do the karate moves!

THANKS, MR. LAWRENCE! I GOT GOOD AT KARATE BY PRACTICING!

Dear George Bush,

You are what this country needs right now. You have proven your leadership while in office. Texas will miss you, but America will benefit.

It's hard to believe you're the son of that impotent beaurocrat who dropped the ball in Iraq. You're clearly your mother's son, like everyone says. You're the talented Bush, not like your father, George Bush Sr. Who is bad.

Signed,
**O. Johnson
Dover, Del.**

SAY, HERE'S ANOTHER ONE FOR ME! READ IT AND WEEP, FELLAS.

OH.

OH . . .

THANK YOU! THAT'S A VERY NICE LETTER THAT YOU WROTE THAT I READ!

UH . . . THAT'S NOT A LET --

LET IT GO! LEAVE HIM WITH A CRUMB OF DIGNITY!

THE X-PRESIDENTIAL MAILBAG

**P.O. BOX 382
DENVER, COLORADO
WWW.IHATECARTER.COM**

CHAPTER
5

GOOD GRIEF, MORE EVIL

AND SO AMERICA FINDS HERSELF ASSAILED FROM THE HEAVENS, A MOST UNUSUAL POSITION FOR A NATION BLESSED BY GOD!

JUST WHO ARE THESE THRAXONIANS?

WE'VE BEEN RUNNING INFORMATION THROUGH THE X-COMPUTER.

AND WHAT HAVE YOU FOUND?

I'LL TELL YOU WHAT WE'VE FOUND!

THEY'RE A RACE OF COMMUNIST ALIENS FROM THE *TELION GALAXY* TWO MILLION LIGHT YEARS AWAY . . .

THESE ALIENS REPRESENT EVERYTHING WE AS AMERICANS STAND AGAINST . . .

IT'S A WORLD WHERE CHILDREN ARE BROUGHT UP WITHOUT *RELIGION* OR *VALUES* . . .

WELFARE
HOW TO GET ON IT AND STAY ON IT

SHIFTLESSNESS IS A COURSE TAUGHT AT MOST UNIVERSITIES . . .

IN GRADE SCHOOL CHILDREN ARE TAUGHT TO PRAY FOR GOD TO DIE . . .

SILENCE!

HEY!!

OUR OWN PRESIDENT -- A *THONG-BIKINIED ASS!*

REALLY? WHAT COLOR THONG?

"THE PUREST AMERICAN MONUMENT" . . . WE'VE GOT TO FIND OUT WHAT . . .

CAN SOMEONE GET ME A MIRROR?

I'LL BET THOSE VILLAINS KNOW!

WE SHALL PLOT THE DEMISE OF THE X-PRESIDENTS AFTER DINNER!

MMM . . . I USUALLY DON'T LIKE LIMA BEANS. BUT THESE ARE GREAT.

THANKS. I JUST SPRINKLE A LITTLE PEPPER IN MY BUTTER SAUCE. IT'S REALLY EASY.

DO YOU HAVE ANY SKIM MILK?

I THINK ALL WE HAVE IS ONE PERCENT.

THAT'S OK THEN, I'LL JUST HAVE WATER.

I'M SORRY.

IT'S NO PROBLEM. JUST GIVE ME SOME MORE OF THOSE ROLLS AND I'LL BE HAPPY.

សូមមេត្តាយកសាច់មាន់វិញ ។

POL POT'S BRAIN WOULD LIKE MORE CHICKEN.

RRRINNNG

I'LL GET IT!

YOU KNOW WHAT, LET THE MACHINE GET IT. I HATE WHEN THE PHONE RUINS DINNER.

. . . MMFF . . . ME TOO . . . MUMMFFF . . . !!!

MR. ANNAN, WE NEED THE SUPPORT OF THE ENTIRE U.N. DELEGATION!

HAH! *WE* ARE UNITED -- TO *DESTROY* YOU!

EVEN MALTA?

MALTA

63

AND SO AMERICA FINDS HERSELF ASSAILED FROM EVERY CORNER OF SPACE . . .

. . . AND EARTH ITSELF!

FOR WHEN A COUNTRY IS AS NOBLE AS THE UNITED STATES OF AMERICA IT CAN TRUST NO ONE! NOT EVEN OTHER COUNTRIES THAT CLAIM TO BE ALLIES, LIKE CANADA AND HAWAII!

EVEN THOSE LOOKING VAGUELY FOREIGN SHOULD BE SHUNNED AND MOVED AWAY FROM!

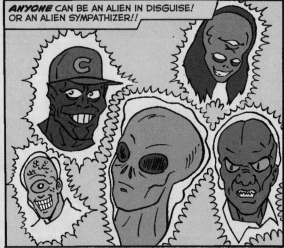

ANYONE CAN BE AN ALIEN IN DISGUISE! OR AN ALIEN SYMPATHIZER!!

WE CALL UPON ALL THE GREATEST AMERICAN HEROES TO JOIN IN THE FINAL BATTLE FOR CHRISTIAN DEMOCRACY! GENERAL SCHWARZKOPF . . .

CLAP CLAP CLAP CLAP CLAP CLAP CLAP CLAP CLAP CLAP CLAP CLAP

64

CHARLTON HESTON . . .

CLAP CLAP
CLAP CLAP
CLAP CLAP
CLAP

EVEL KNIEVEL . . .

CLAP CLAP
CLAP CLAP
CLAP CLAP

OLIVER NORTH . . .

CLAP
CLAP
CLAP

BERNHARD GOETZ . . .

CLAP
COUGH CLAP

CLAP

MAY GOD BE WITH ALL OF YOU.

CLAP
CLAP
CLAP
CLAP

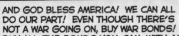

AND GOD BLESS AMERICA! WE CAN ALL DO OUR PART! EVEN THOUGH THERE'S NOT A WAR GOING ON, BUY WAR BONDS! BUY ALL THE BONDS YOU CAN, WITH ANY MONEY YOU CAN FIND OR STEAL!! JOIN YOUR LOCAL U.S.O.! COME ON, YOU LAZY SACKS OF SHIT!

I LOVE THIS COUNTRY!! I LOVE THIS NATION!! LET'S ALL GET BEHIND OUR BOYS IN GERMANY!!

ARMED WITH A NEW THINK TANK OF HEROES, THE X-PRESIDENTS HUDDLE IN CHARLTON HESTON'S LAIR TO ANTICIPATE EVIL'S NEXT MOVE . . .

LIVE FROM DISNEY WORLD

66

AND SO, AMERICA FACES HER WORST NIGHTMARE AS ANIMATRONS, FREED FROM THIRTY-FIVE YEARS OF REPETITIVE MOTIONS, WREAK HAVOC IN THE GUISE OF OUR MOST *HALLOWED FATHERS OF FREEDOM!*

72

THE *FUCK STOPS HERE!*

GAS

FOUR SCORE AND SEVEN YEARS AGO I KICKED THE SHIT OUT OF YOU!

WAIT, THAT'S NOT YOURS!

GIVE ME A BREAK, I'M BENJAMIN HARRISON!

LOSING ENERGY AND BATTLING THEIR EVIL SELVES TO A HOPELESS STANDOFF, OUR HEROES FALL BACK ON AMERICAN INGENUITY!

I'VE DETERMINED THAT THIS IS NOT A WINNABLE CONFLICT. LET'S PULL BACK AND BOMB CAMBODIA AGAIN.

HENRY, YOU'RE INSANE. BUT IT GIVES ME AN IDEA. THERE IS SOMETHING WE CAN HIT -- *THE COMMAND SHIP!*

IF WE TAKE IT ON TOGETHER, IT MIGHT *DISABLE* THE ANIMATRONS!

LET'S DO IT!

YEAH!

73

74

AND SO, THE X-PRESIDENTS RETURN AMERICA TO SAFETY, REMINDING US OF WHAT MAKES HER GREAT...

FOR AMERICA NEEDS MORE THAN HER PRESIDENTS, HER SUPERHEROES, HER MONUMENTS AND HER ANIMATRONS TO STAY AHEAD.

WE CAN *ALL* PITCH IN TO KEEP OUR NATION'S STANDARD OF LIVING FAR BETTER . . .

THAN ANY OTHER NATION ON EARTH . . .

. . . AND *WAY* BETTER THAN THIRD WORLD NATIONS!

THANKS TO ALL OF YOU, THE WORLD IS FINALLY AT PEACE!

EXCEPT FOR KOSOVO, THE MIDDLE EAST, RWANDA, PAKISTAN, CHINA, AND OUR INNER CITIES.

WE'RE SORRY YOU'RE STILL AN ASSHEAD.

WITH OUR PRAYERS AND THE MODERATES' MOMENT OF SILENCE, IT'LL WEAR OFF IN TIME.

THAT'S ALRIGHT. AT LEAST I KNOW WHO HE'S SITTING ON!

HA HA HA HA HA HA

76

ASSORTED ANNOUNCEMENTS AND ANECDOTES
ALL ABOUT ALLITERATIVE ARTISTS AND ALKIES

ROBERT SMIGEL'S SOAPBOX

All right, gang. Time for Yeroyal Robness to wipe off some egg. Seems like everyone in comicdom spotted our "goof" in the last ish. We gave Jimmy Carter a RED tie on p. 45 -- and everyone in Randomdom knows the X-P favors BLUE. Talk about egg -- this time I got the whole chicken! Mea Culpa AND Farrow! But, hey, we folks here at Random House Comics have got lives, too! And major happenings! A buddy asked me to circulate a little bit of his cash through my income tax return, suddenly I got Perry Mason yelling in my ear! I mean, I grew up with this yike in my neighborhood -- and now I'm looking at a jail stint and possibly losing the mag! The only thing that loves me back! But we all got probs, right gang? Hey, the editors say if you're under 15 don't read on -- but YerRobness found a little blood in his semen! Staring at your mortality during what oughta be a sexual moment makes it kinda hard to remember what kind of tie Jimmy Carter wore! But don't fret, gang, it coulda come from numerous things. Maybe it came from all that wood alcohol I'd been consuming lately. Or those Irish kids that kneed me in the nuts after I was a little too "friendly" with their sister! Hey, she said she liked the last ish! All I know for sure is, there's blood in that thar semen! I'm trying to be lighthearted about it, but I'm really terrified! And to top it off, YerRob's daughter's dating a Puerto Rican! Nothing against the Puerto Ricans, but you just know when they have a fight, it's the first thing that's gonna come out. So we're sorry we got Carter's tie wrong, gang! We'll try to be PERFECT next ish! Keep the letters and the pressure comin'!

ADAM MCKAY'S SOAPBOX

Hey, X-P heads, thanks for keeping us honest with the Jimmy Carter tie! Your input helps us stay ahead of the competish! But maybe you wanna lay off YerRobness for a spell! Let me lay some other info on you. Rob caught his wife walking out of a Radisson with Wayne Chrebet! Now he's all worried about being a "Comic book" guy. He's been drawing correct Jimmy Carter ties all over the walls of his office in magic marker all week between snorting Vivarin. He doesn't need criticism from little dorks whose idea of pain is their wiffle ball skittering under the bushes and who took the last Otter Pop. Rob goes home and hears dirty answering machine messages from Jerome Bettis. They don't even care that he's home! Sure, Bettis is *good* -- I blame Pittsburgh's offensive line eroding for his dropoff -- but this is rough, gang! Y'know, I'm going to stop saying "gang" and "ish" for a moment and speak to you straight. He's a dear, lovely man who's under a lot of stress. And there's blood in his semen. Give him a fucking break. You pimple-faced fags. Ten years ago he was one of the most creative people I've ever known. You know what's it's like to watch a close friend spiritually die right in front in you? So the next time you notice Ronald Reagan is wearing the wrong belt buckle, or Gerald Ford has a mustache, or Jimmy Carter has breasts -- and let me tell you, the next issue has a whole lot more mistakes! There's mixed-up heads, men crying, pigeon-like scrawl about the walls closing in. Just give him a pass on this one! Okay, "gang"? Holy Jesus, I know you're all just 12, but hear me! Every morning I'm showering till my skin is raw. It's bad around here! The guys over at DC are laughing at us. Fuck DC. I have to watch my friend and mentor sitting in his underwear with zipper boots passed out on the floor cradling a photo album of his wife and kids. There's your fucking no-prize!

Additional thanks to:

Adrian Urquidez, Roy Richardson, Rob Issen, David Margolies, David Lipson, Luciano DiGeronimo, Aaron Casper, Derek Santiago, Lee Stacy, Joe Goldberg, Gideon Kendall, Sharon Marianetti, J.J. Sedelmaier, Dick Ayers and Rich Ayers.

For Michelle and Daniel, Shira and Lily, Barbara, Alli and Josh, Brett, Zack and Max.

Library of Congress
Cataloging-in-Publication Data

Smigel, Robert.
X-Presidents by Robert Smigel and Adam McKay; illustrations by Wachtenheim/Marianetti Animation
p. cm
ISBN 0-679-78362-8
I. McKay, Adam. II. Title.
PN6727.S545 X67 2000   741.5'973-
dc21   00-027579

Villard website address: www.villard.com
Printed in the United States of America on acid-free paper
24689753
First Edition

Book designed by
Wachtenheim/ Marianetti Animation

ITEM! Hey, we've been promising and promising to give you the scoop on our new title from DAVID "Holiday" WACHTENHEIM just as soon as the time was right. It's ELIAN, and the first ish is a guaranteed fly-off-the-shelfer! Our pint-sized pinata-lover is bitten by a radioactive porpoise and grows to 300 pounds! *Now* who has to go back? With the cable-newsies still dishing the dirt on our favorite Cuban this side of Ricky Ricardo, this ought to be David's biggest hit yet! We're betting that if you dig the real Elian, this just *has* to be your bag of phantasmagorical fun! It *has* to! I mean, give the goddam cretins what they want, right? ELIAN comes out next month, and it figures to go through the roof! It really does!

ITEM! Hope you're digging the grooves laid down by ROB "Not a Puppet" MARIANETTI in this month's ish of MARIA SHRIVER. Rob and the crew are just warmin' up! Check out his work with Cool CHRIS KNOWLES in next month's MARIA SHRIVER GIANT SIZED ANNUAL. Rob and Chris just jammed a weekend's worth of wizardry at ROB "Tape House" ISSEN's rural retreat and came back with the wildest action sketches since SHRIVER #289.

ITEM! We had to call in the big gun, Marvelous MIKE WETTERHAHN, to handle the pencils for the next big ish of MUMIA. Our did-he-or-didn't-he superstar is on the loose! As all Randomites know, he broke out of jail in MUMIA #93. Now he's swimming into the river and taking on the Great Blue Whale -- and only Ed Asner can save him! This is one MUMIA that's so good *it* should be put to death!

ITEM! Is anyone else out there in Randomdom just incredibly disappointed with their own children? And how they turned out? It's just damn life-numbing, ain't it?

ITEM! Hold on to your cowls, Randomheads, because you're not gonna believe it! Our big new title MILLENNIUM Y2K is finally ready to roll after some production delays and jillions of letters from you good people. What will happen when the Millennium hits? It's far beyond anything you feared would happen when you were worried about it. Yep, there'll be no better comic to read as you anticipate reminiscing about worrying about what would happen. With the steady hand of inker JOE "I Fucking Blew It" RUBINSTEIN and penciler KEVIN "I Swear it's Joe's Fault" KOBASIC, the 14-issue monthly will count you down to the dreaded year 2002. What will happen when the clock hits *that* year? You haven't even thought about it, have you?! Well, you'd better start!!!! Please?

ITEM! BOB "Bippy" SUAREZ takes over the pencils for next month's THREE TENORS just in time for Carreras to finally settle the Kree-Skrull war! And that's ANDREW "Andrew" COVALT doing the snazzy new lettering in BIG HUGE HAIRY DICK #95, with a special appearance by Captain Justice. And let's close out our parade of plugola with a warm goodbye to DAVID DINKINS' WORLD OF ACTION.